HIGH-TECH CAREERS

Careers in Gaming

Laura Roberts

ReferencePoint
Press®

For more information, contact:
ReferencePoint Press, Inc.
PO Box 27779
San Diego, CA 92198
www.ReferencePointPress.com

LIBRARY OF CONGRESS CATALOGING-IN-PUBLICATION DATA

Names: Roberts, Laura
Title: Careers in gaming / by Laura Roberts.
Description: San Diego, CA : ReferencePoint Press, Inc., [2017] | Series: High-tech careers | Includes bibliographical references and index. | Audience: Grades 9 to 12.
Identifiers: LCCN 2016035292 (print) | LCCN 2016035645 (ebook) | ISBN 9781682821121 (hardback) | ISBN 9781682821138 (eBook)
Subjects: LCSH: Computer games--Programming--Vocational guidance--Juvenile literature. | Computer games--Design--Vocational guidance--Juvenile literature.
Classification: LCC QA76.76.C672 R6326 2017 (print) | LCC QA76.76.C672 (ebook) | DDC 794.8/1536023--dc23
LC record available at https://lccn.loc.gov/2016035292

Contents

The Ever-Expanding Video Game Industry

The video game industry is growing faster than ever before. More and more Americans are packing computing power in their pockets with powerful cell phones and tablets. Some even access the Internet as frequently to play games as they do to check their e-mail. As a result of all this online activity, the gaming industry is growing exponentially. As staffer Dylan Lewis states on the financial topics website Motley Fool, "The worldwide mobile gaming market is a high $20 billion market. I've seen projections that that will hit $45 billion by 2018." And as the demand for games continues to grow, this means jobs for game developers, designers, animators, programmers, and many more in the gaming industry will expand too.

No longer solely the domain of teenagers playing on consoles in their bedroom or their family's basement, modern video games have expanded their reach. *The 2016 Essential Facts About the Computer and Video Game Industry* report states that "the average video game player is 35 years old and has been playing video games for about 13 years." Video games attract older players too. According to a June 2016 Entertainment Software Association study, "Three-quarters of gamers age 50-plus play weekly, with four in 10 playing daily. Among gamers age 60 and above, 43 percent play video games every day."

The recently released *Pokémon Go* is even getting gamers out of the house and interacting with the world around them (to the tune of 9.55 million users, daily, according to a July 13, 2016, article on the website Recode). Offering a blend of virtual and actual reality dubbed *augmented reality*, the game requires users to physically walk to various landmarks in their city in order to advance game play, making exercise a core ingredient not just for participation but for success within the game. The gamification of our culture continues unabated, as the geeks of yesterday continue to become the leaders of today.

Changes Bode Well for Workers

Though the gaming industry has been male dominated since its inception, things are changing. Women have begun joining the ranks of game industry professionals and are likely to be a big part of the industry in the future. In a May 2016 interview with CBS News, Stephen Wood, a Moore College of Art & Design gaming arts professor from Philadelphia, commented,

> There's going to be a huge boom of women entering the industry in the next 10 years. In the '80s and '90s, video games were seen as things boys do. But in the '90s and early 2000s, girls said, 'We're going to play, too.' Now those girls are going to college and studying video games. We're helping close that gender gap and being part of the solution.

Despite—or perhaps because of—Gamergate (a 2014 scandal in which female game developers like Zoë Quinn and Brianna Wu were specifically targeted for harassment online), young women are eager to join the video game industry, and the educational system is eager to accommodate their interests. As more women join the ranks of programmers and developers, the industry continues to become more welcoming, and women in design careers are beginning to enjoy the same success as their male counterparts.

Though the Bureau of Labor Statistics does not track jobs in the video game industry specifically, it is clear that this particular corner of the tech world is booming. With approximately 2.6 billion gamers worldwide, playing on an astounding array of platforms, the video game industry is simply exploding. This bodes well for job seekers.

The Major Areas of Study

The video game industry is a great choice for students interested in a wide variety of academic fields. Combining elements of fine art, computer technology and design, game theory, music, psychology, and sociology, video games incorporate multimedia disciplines from across a wide spectrum. Artists and engineers alike are welcome in the video

Careers in Gaming

Job Title	Role
Animator	Game animators are responsible for the portrayal of movement and behavior within a game
Assistant Producer	Assistant producers work with a game's production staff to ensure the timely delivery of the product
Audio Engineer	Game audio engineers create the sound track for a game, including music, sound effects, character voices, and spoken instructions
Creative Director	Creative directors are responsible for the overall look and feel of a computer game
Development and Operations (DevOps) Engineer	DevOps engineers are responsible for creating an online infrastructure for a game, and ensuring the stability and security of the web services
External Producer	External producers ensure the successful delivery of a game while working externally from the game development team
Game Designer/ Developer	Game designers devise what a game consists of and how it plays, defining all the core elements
Lead Programmer	Lead programmers manage the programming team responsible for creating all the game's computer code
Game Programmer	Game programmers design and write the computer code that runs and controls a game
Lead Game Artist	Lead artists are responsible for the overall look of a game
Game Artist	Games artists create the visual elements of a game, such as characters, scenery, objects, vehicles, surface textures, and clothing
Level Editor	Level editors define and create interactive architecture for a segment of a game, including the landscape, buildings, and objects

Source: Creative Skillset, "Job Roles," 2016. www.creativeskillset.org.

game industry, and most end up collaborating on projects rather than working in isolation as in other careers.

Fine artists may find work as animators; character artists or modelers; concept, environment, technical, texture, or lighting artists; or art directors. Programmers may find themselves involved with engine, game play, physics, user interface, or artificial intelligence programming. The musically inclined could find jobs in the industry as audio programmers or engineers, composers, voice-over artists, or even Foley (sound effects) artists. Writers, designers, developers, and many more staff are also required to create video games that will amuse, educate, and enchant players.

A Competitive Field

Although the video game industry is certainly welcoming of a wide variety of disciplines and career directions, it is also a highly competitive field. Part of the reason for this is its obvious draw: playing video games for a living. But, of course, there is much more to it than that, and although working for a gaming company can certainly be fun, there is also plenty of hard work involved.

Cross-discipline STEAM (science, technology, engineering, art, and math) degrees come in handy in the industry, but it will take more than good grades to get a foot in the door. What employers are really looking for is a passion for video games and gaming as well as the creative ability to build new games. As John Newcomer, the creative director at Reliance Games, mentions in a recent interview with Digital-Tutors .com, "I want to see a twinkle in the candidate's eye that they're in this business because they want to be. There's a joy and passion to create games and entertainment. I want to know if the person has creative ability and how universal it is. They need to be able to dissect a game and tell me why it's fun or successful. What makes it tick?" Newcomer also notes that although knowledge of an array of digital tools, from Photoshop to Maya LT (and many more), is important, what is even more crucial to any new hire's success is his or her ability to communicate with the other members of the team. Combining soft skills like the ability to work well in groups, technical ability, and creativity is often just the right blend required for success in the video game industry.

Game Developer

Game developers (or game designers) wear many hats. The bulk of their job is to establish a game's plot and develop its characters. Different types of games will necessarily have different types of plots and characters. For example, whereas first-person shooter games typically follow military or postapocalyptic story lines that require physical fighting to advance, quest games often involve solving puzzles to move forward in the game. The type of game usually dictates what kinds of characters will appear, offering players different personas with assorted traits that can help them succeed in the game. Game developers are responsible for designing different types of quests for players to embark upon, creating the levels for players to work through, writing story lines for characters to follow and dialogue for characters to say during the game, and even creating the mechanics of the game to make it run as planned. Developers are, ultimately, responsible for designing everything from characters to levels and puzzles to art and animation. According to an Econsultancy.com interview with Pete Low, a game designer at Chunk,

At a Glance:

Game Developer

Minimum Educational Requirements
Bachelor's or associate's degree

Personal Qualities
Creativity and storytelling skills; problem-solving ability; team player; strong written communication skills

Working Conditions
Indoors

Salary Range
About $58,253 to $100,690

Number of Jobs
As of 2014 about 1.1 million

Future Job Outlook
Growth rate of 14 percent or higher through 2024

A game developer, or designer, creates a story and its characters. The developer also oversees how all of the components of the game—including the story line, characters, rules, environments, and game play experience—come together.

Game design is the process of designing the content and rules of a game; the gameplay, environments, storyline and characters. A games designer may specialize in one category (level design, writing, balancing difficulty) or all depending on the size and complexity of the project. There are many components that go into making video games: art, animation, audio and user interface design. There can be script writing, creating systems of economy within the product itself, the wide variety of potential social components and more. It's my job to see how all of these can come together to achieve the game's goals—and then be able to communicate this vision to a wide variety of stakeholders.

Developers may also be involved in coding software, art direction, or graphic design. They may even be involved in beta testing prerelease versions of the game before sending it on to quality assurance testers. Depending on the size of the studio they work for, some parts of a developer's job may also be similar to the role of a producer or director in the film industry, such as keeping the project on track and delivering the finished game to consumers on time.

Different types of game developers will be responsible for different aspects of game play. Game mechanics designers make sure that the rules of the game are properly defined, and environmental designers devise many different scenes (or environments) in which the game can be played. Lead designers coordinate all of the individual designers and help direct communication within the team. As leaders, they must also take charge to make important decisions about the game as a whole. For example, Tom, a lead designer at Firemonkeys Studios (part of EA Games), notes on the EA Games website that "as a lead, I have a sizeable say in the project's long-term direction. I also do a bunch of mentoring and helping people to achieve their career goals. It always gives me a thrill when one of the designers on my team has a great idea, creates some sweet content, or comes up with a clever solution to a problem. Makes me proud!"

How Do You Become a Game Developer?

Education
Students looking for a job as a game developer should strongly consider a degree or certificate in game design; this degree will focus on the skills most often required for game design and development, including knowledge of game theory, game planning, and strategy. Creative writing degrees can also prove useful as game designers must be strong storytellers with excellent character development skills. According to O*NET OnLine which groups game developers with software developers, about 62 percent of software developers have a bachelor's degree, 19 percent have an associate's degree, and 17 percent have attended some college but possess no degree.

Internships
Would-be video game developers should definitely apply for internships with video game companies that match their skills and

ambitions. Not only will an internship help provide valuable experience, but it can also be a foot in the door of the ultracompetitive gaming industry. Most, if not all, of these opportunities are paid internships, and some even include housing stipends or arrangements and cover participants' travel expenses. Blizzard Entertainment offers college students a chance to join its twelve-week summer internships, which take place at one of the company's three US locations (Austin, Texas; Irvine, California; or San Francisco, California). PlayStation also offers twelve-week summer internships, which are open to both undergraduate and graduate students.

Skills and Personality

Game developers are creative types with a passion to share their ideas for games and create entirely new worlds from scratch. Developers are also storytellers. They need strong storyboarding abilities to convey their vision to the design team through drawings of various scenes that need to appear in the game. Developers are also computer programmers with coding skills, which means they must strike the right balance of creativity and computer science. As part of finding this balance, developers need to be able to analyze creative suggestions as well as the practicality of achieving them—and all without losing sight of the intended audience. An article on the game review and news website ZTGD describes the qualities that make a successful game developer. Successful developers are those who ask themselves questions like

> Who is the player? What type of game is the intended outcome? . . . Game design will vary greatly depending on the answer to these two questions. Good analytical skills will help answer these questions and is the next favorable characteristic game developers are looking for. Being able to determine what part of the game is and is not working is important to a promising result. Video game players are looking for a game that grabs their attention right away and holds it.

The most successful developers are able to work well as part of a team. Game design requires many different moving parts and

11

specialized abilities, so being able to express ideas clearly is very important. Developers must work with fellow designers, coders, artists, animators, and more to create a game, so being able to understand where each member of the team is coming from is critical for solving problems.

Problem-solving skills and patience are also core traits for game developers. They must remain flexible creatively and financially, offering solutions to problems that arise and keeping the entire project moving forward. Being able to keep calm to work through these challenges is essential. Work hours can often be long, which may cause frayed nerves, so patience with fellow team members—especially when on deadlines—is very important.

Developers must also possess managerial skills since they are both producers and directors of a game's overall production. Developers often take up the tasks of managing the budget, organizing the team's work schedules, and keeping projects on schedule in order to hit various milestones as well as the final deadline.

On the Job

Employers

Game developers may work for top studios, such as Ubisoft, Nintendo, Sony, EA Games, or Blizzard. These developers are responsible for the majority of the video games available for consoles and mobile devices. In addition, there are many freelance game developers; these developers are self-employed and run their own businesses or may work on developing games in their free time. Brianna Wu and Amanda Warner are independent game developers and cofounders of Giant Spacekat. On the company's website they note that they create games "where the women [are] the heroes, not an afterthought." Dave Castlenuovo, the sole programmer at Bolt Creative, is another freelancer. The perks, as Castlenuovo puts it in an interview with the website All Things D, come from the company's indie status: "We made a decision to stay small. To me, I get the most enjoyment working out of my home, getting to see my wife."

As a 2014 *VentureBeat* article explains, more and more high-profile developers are making the move from larger companies to setting up their own shops, and it seems that this trend will continue in the future. Joseph Humfrey, art and code director for Inkle studios, adds, in an Indie Game Reviewer article, "Platforms like Steam and the App Store have created a blossoming market, and tools like Unity have leveled the playing field for developers of different backgrounds and years of experience. You no longer need a vast team to build a technically and visually impressive game."

Working Conditions

Game developers typically work in office or studio environments, alongside fellow designers and programmers. Developers may have their own office or cubicle, or there may be an open floor plan in order to facilitate group work. Most developers work full-time, and there are typically many overtime hours logged as well.

Independent game developers may also work on their days off, over lunch breaks, or on weekends to collaborate with teammates working in other cities around the world. As Emeric Thoa, creative director for the Game Bakers, describes life as an indie for the website Indie Game Reviewer, "It's like being in a music band. You can be successful and admired like an artist and a star, or you can go from small gig to small gig, hoping it takes off one day. But in both cases it's very satisfying and tiring at the same time."

Earnings

The salary of video game developers depends on the type of company they work for as well as the skills and experience they have amassed on the job. According to O*NET OnLine, which groups video game developers in with software developers, at one end of the spectrum are beginning designers, who earn about $63,970 to $73,864 a year. At the other end are more advanced designers, who can earn between $98,260 and $100,690 per year. According to information obtained by the job search website Indeed in July 2016, typical video game designers make an average of $58,253 per year.

Opportunities for Advancement

Video game developer is not an entry-level job; therefore, there is not much room for advancing to higher-level positions. However, developers can learn additional skills on the job and can receive pay bumps as they add skills and take on greater responsibilities. Or they can start their own companies, independently producing and publishing their own games. Although this option carries the most risk since developers must be able to do everything themselves (or hire staff to help with things they cannot), it also holds the opportunity for the greatest reward—particularly if a developer's games go viral or strike a chord within the gaming community.

What Is the Future Outlook for Game Developers?

Game developers have a bright future. There is a predicted growth rate of 14 percent or higher through 2024, according to O*NET. This is considered much faster than average. O*NET also projects 238,000 job openings for the same time period (through 2024), which means it is a great time to get in on the ground floor of the video game industry and work your way up to the level of developer. Consumers continue to have an insatiable thirst for new games; therefore, developers will always have plenty of jobs for the taking.

Find Out More

Game Center
http://gamecenter.nyu.edu

The website of New York University's Game Center, part of its Department of Game Design, has information about academic coursework and exhibitions, game design workshops, competitions, and conferences. It also provides information on the university's Game Center Incubator, which helps students develop their games for the marketplace.

Game Industry Career Guide
www.gameindustrycareerguide.com

This is an information hub for video game career seekers, offering lots of practical advice for landing a job in the industry. Game industry careers are profiled in detail; and students can also find information about writing résumés, applying for jobs, networking, and interviewing.

Kotaku
www.kotaku.com

Both professionals and avid gamers present news and opinions about video games here. This site is a good place to find out about lots of different games—without having to actually purchase and play them all—as well as to keep track of the latest industry news through some of its biggest fans.

Values at Play
www.valuesatplay.org

This website is aimed at helping designers to be more intentional about integrating diversity and human values into games and game-based systems. Students can explore game tools and curriculum, conduct research, explore resources, and watch video interviews with experts in the field.

We Are Game Devs
www.wearegamedevs.com

This website celebrates diversity in the video game industry and features extended interviews with game developers, designers, artists, animators, programmers, and more. Women and people of color are specifically highlighted, with the aim of promoting and expanding the industry's inclusion of them. Readers can also help steer the discussion by making suggestions for new developers to interview.

Game Mechanics Designer

Game mechanics designers, also known as systems designers, create the rules and systems for interacting within a game. This work is what makes game play possible. As Jesse Schell, founder of Schell Games, explains in his book *The Art of Game Design: A Book of Lenses*: "These are the procedures and rules of your game. Mechanics describe the goal of your game, how players can and cannot try to achieve it, and what happens when they try."

All games, not just video games, operate with rules. Sharon Boller, in her online article "Learning Game Design Series, Part 3: Game Mechanics," cites the Monopoly rule—"When players pass Go, they collect $200"—as an example of an explicit rule (or mechanic) that players follow. In a video game, a rule or mechanic is programmed into the game. Boller gives an example: "When players respond incorrectly to a question they get immediate feedback on what a correct response should be, followed by an opportunity to re-try answering the question."

At a Glance:

Game Mechanics Designer

Minimum Educational Requirements
Bachelor's or associate's degree

Personal Qualities
Creativity and storytelling skills; problem-solving ability; team player; strong written communication skills

Working Conditions
Indoors

Salary Range
About $63,970 to $100,690

Number of Jobs
As of 2014 about 1.1 million

Future Job Outlook
Growth rate of 14 percent or higher through 2024

Not all game mechanics designers do the same thing. For instance, those who work on fighting games are called combat designers, and their job is to create a coherent system for what occurs when two or more characters fight. Game mechanics designers may also hold titles based on the type of work they do, including level designers, achievement designers, world builders, mission or quest designers, economy designers, and puzzle designers.

The main task of a game mechanics designer is to create engaging experiences for players. Sometimes these experiences are simple and fun, but other times they are incredibly difficult or even frustrating. Regardless of difficulty, the goal is to make sure a player will want to continue playing the game. More difficult games usually offer more significant rewards for beating a level, which is what encourages users to continue playing. Designers use a variety of psychological techniques and game design theories to encourage players to push forward, even when the going gets tough. Different approaches help designers create well-crafted games and unique experiences that players deem worthy of their time. This might include the carrot-and-stick approach, in which players are either rewarded for correct actions with a carrot, or valuable item, or punished for incorrect actions by a beating with a stick, or other negative experience. As game design expert Amy Jo Kim explains in an interview with the website Bokardo, "Game mechanics are a collection of tools and systems that an interactive designer can use to make an experience more fun and compelling. . . . These core mechanics are a good place to start: collecting, points, feedback, exchange, and customization."

Game mechanics can be complex or simple, depending on the type of game, and both types can create great game play experiences if properly done. Video games played on computers and consoles typically use more complex mechanics than games played on a cell phone or tablet, as they are more dependent on a computer's processing speed. There are also usually several different types of mechanics at play in any given game. For example, as the "Beginner's Guide to Game Mechanics" at GameDesigning.org explains, *Tetris* (a game that can be played on multiple platforms) involves four different types of game mechanics:

1. Rotation system: Where the tetrominoes [puzzle pieces] spawn, in what position they spawn, how they rotate, and their wall kick (their position when you try to rotate on the edge). 2. Randomizers: The order/sequence in which the tetromino types spawn. 3. Scoring Systems: The points you get for line clears, including back-to-back lines, combos, T-spins, etc. 4. Mobility: The player's ability to manipulate the tetrominoes, including rotating, dropping, etc.

The guide goes on to suggest that "if you're an aspiring game designer, one of the best exercises you can do is take any game and try to break it down into main game mechanics." This exercise helps would-be designers understand exactly what makes any game tick and how they can begin to assemble complex or simple games of their own.

How Do You Become a Game Mechanics Designer?

Education

An ideal field of study for would-be game mechanics designers is computer science or video game design. Most colleges and universities offer computer science degree programs. The top four schools for computer science, according to the *U.S. News & World Report*, are Carnegie Mellon University, the Massachusetts Institute of Technology, Stanford University, and the University of California, Berkeley, although there are many other similar programs in universities throughout the United States. These four-year programs introduce students to the core concepts of game design, including classes in programming, story and character development, visual and sound design, and game engine development. Earning a degree in computer science exposes would-be designers to information about various operating systems, programming concepts, input/output methods, and algorithms.

Video game design programs are still few in number, but the best-known ones are at the Art Institute, the University of Southern California, Carnegie Mellon University, the University of Utah, and the

Rochester Institute of Technology. The University of Utah's program boasts a strong relationship with EA Sports, headquartered in Salt Lake City. The Rochester Institute of Technology offers more than 150 classes a year, along with several different types of game design and development degrees. Additional fields of study useful for game mechanics design are formal logic and mathematics; these fields will help aspiring designers understand and improve their programming skills. A strong grasp of physics is also important when designing a game's mechanics and environment. According to O*NET, about 62 percent of game designers have a bachelor's degree, 19 percent have an associate's degree, and 17 percent have attended some college but possess no degree.

Internships

Would-be game mechanics designers should definitely apply for internships with video game companies that match their skills and ambitions. Not only will an internship help provide valuable experience, but it can also be a foot in the door of the ultracompetitive gaming industry. Most, if not all, of these opportunities are paid internships, and some even include housing stipends or arrangements and cover participants' travel expenses. Blizzard Entertainment offers college students a chance to join their twelve-week summer internships, which take place at one of the company's three US locations (Austin, Texas; Irvine, California; or San Francisco, California). PlayStation also offers twelve-week summer internships, which are open to both undergraduate and graduate students.

Skills and Personality

Game mechanics designers are computer programmers with strong coding skills as well as problem solvers. Being able to think through difficult questions and come up with innovative solutions is key to a game mechanics designer's success. They must remain flexible in their thinking, offering solutions to problems that arise in order to keep the project moving forward. Being able to keep calm to work through these challenges is essential. Work hours can often be long, which may cause frayed nerves, so patience with fellow team members— especially when on deadlines—is very important.

The most successful mechanics designers are able to work well as part of a team. Game design requires many different moving parts and specialized abilities, so being able to express ideas clearly is important. Mechanics designers must work with fellow designers, coders, artists, animators, developers, and more to create a game, so being able to understand where each member of the team is coming from is critical for solving problems. As game designer Jake Fleming explained during a 2014 Treehouse website interview,

> When the [team feels] good about any particular idea, we start developing a prototype with basic colored shapes to show to friends, family, and even strangers. We can get a sense for just how fun our core game mechanic can be without fancy art and music clouding the user's judgment. Showing the game to everyone who will listen and quickly iterating based on their feedback is how we know when we want to take an idea to the next level.

On the Job

Employers

Game mechanics designers may work for top studios, such as Ubisoft, Nintendo, Sony, EA Games, or Blizzard. These designers are responsible for the majority of the video games available for consoles and mobile devices. In addition, there are also many freelance designers who are self-employed but contract out their work to different studios.

Working Conditions

Game mechanics designers typically work in office or studio environments, alongside fellow designers and programmers. Designers may have their own office or cubicle, or there may be an open floor plan in order to facilitate group work. Most designers work full-time, and there are typically many overtime hours logged as well.

Working conditions can vary drastically according to a designer's wants and needs. In a July 2015 interview on Medium.com, independent artist and game designer Kara Stone talked about her workplace and its effect on her work: "I mostly work at home surrounded by plants, burning incense, spending a lot of time away from my computer lying on the ground thinking. Not feeling forced to sit in front of a screen and having my hippie surroundings makes the process and the outcome a little more serene, personal, thoughtful." In short, most designers want and require their own particular time and space to figure out the mechanics and assorted issues related to the games they are working on. Fortunately for them, most successful video game companies allow them that time and space.

Earnings

The salary of game mechanics designers depends on the type of company they work for and the skills and experience they have amassed on the job. According to O*NET and the Bureau of Labor Statistics, at one end of the spectrum are beginning designers, who earn about $63,970 to $73,864 a year. At the other end are more advanced designers, who can earn between $98,260 and $100,690 per year. According to information obtained by the job search website Indeed in July 2016, typical game designers make an average of $87,000 per year.

Opportunities for Advancement

Game mechanics designer is not an entry-level job, and therefore there is not much room for advancing to higher-level positions. However, mechanic designers can learn additional skills on the job and can receive pay bumps as they add skills and take on greater responsibilities. Or they can start their own companies, independently producing and publishing their own games. Although this option carries the most risk since designers must be able to do everything themselves (or hire staff to help with things they cannot), it also holds the opportunity for the greatest reward—particularly if a designer's games go viral or strike a chord within the gaming community.

What Is the Future Outlook for Game Mechanics Designers?

Game mechanics designers have a very bright future. According to O*NET, there is a predicted growth rate of 14 percent or higher through 2024, which is designated as much faster than average. There are 238,000 projected job openings for the same time period, which means it is a great time to get in on the ground floor of the video game industry and work your way up to the level of designer. Consumers continue to have an insatiable thirst for new games; therefore, designers will always have plenty of jobs for the taking.

Find Out More

Develop Online
www.develop-online.net

This European-based website details the latest business, coding, art, sound, and game design trends, and covers creative and commercial leaders in the field. The site is intended for use by creatives currently working in the gaming industry, and it does not shy away from technical subjects or industry issues.

Game Sauce
www.gamesauce.biz

Use this website to follow game development news from around the world, including exclusive interviews, studio spotlights, video coverage, and more.

Gamestar Mechanic
www.gamestarmechanic.com

This website is devoted to helping people learn to design video games by using game-based quests and courses. Although the site is aimed at kids aged seven to fourteen, it is also open to anyone who wants to learn more about game design.

Indie Games
www.indiegames.com

A resource for indie game designers and developers, this site explores games produced and developed by independent designers. Read reviews of new games and reports on the state of the indie gaming industry, and keep up with the work of fellow designers.

The Independent Gaming Source
www.tigsource.com

Independent Gaming Source is a community of independent game developers and players. The site's forums are a popular hangout for indie developers and players to chat about their favorite games and how to improve them, announce Kickstarter projects, or find local meetups and developer events.

Programmer

Video game programmers do the hard work behind the scenes: they create all of the code that makes games run smoothly. The Game Career Guide website describes the job of a programmer in the video game industry this way:

At a Glance:

Programmer

Minimum Educational Requirements
Bachelor's or associate's degree

Personal Qualities
Critical-thinking, problem-solving, and strong written and oral communication skills; team player

Certification
Required

Working Conditions
Indoors

Salary Range
About $77,550 to $102,000

Number of Jobs
As of 2014 about 328,600

Future Job Outlook
Rate of growth is declining as jobs shift overseas

At the most basic level, programmers write the code that makes things happen in a video game. This includes connecting or "mapping" the player input from the control pad to the action that's happening on the screen. It also includes all the action or movement of non-player characters [NPC]; for instance, when you see NPCs wandering the terrain of a video game, it's the programmers who gave the characters the artificial intelligence to roam where they do.

Programmers typically specialize in one of several areas.

Artificial intelligence (AI) programmers decide how the characters in a game will react in response to different actions performed by a human player on his or her computer. Some examples of this include strategy (decision-making algorithms, which calculate the pros and cons of taking one action versus another), pathfinding (plotting the shortest route between two points in the game), and enemy tactics (the types of actions a game's villain can take to improve his or her position within the game). Different coding scripts are used to program these reactions, and AI programmers are typically well versed in several different computer languages.

Physics programmers make the rules that govern the game world, including effects like gravity and the way characters interact with objects. These programmers also control special effects, including explosions, fire, and laser beams. Characters' bodies are also subject to the laws of physics, so programmers will be in charge of creating effects for bodies hitting the ground or suffering impacts of other kinds, which are usually referred to as so-called ragdoll physics.

Graphics programmers focus on using colors, shading, light, shadows, and textures to give players visual cues about what they are supposed to do in each scene. They work to give two-dimensional art a feeling of being three-dimensional, and they also help to compress data so that there is no lag time within a game as it is played.

User interface programmers write code that runs the game engine. In other words, this kind of programming is responsible for how players navigate through the game. Navigation typically uses some type of menu system to control everything from choosing a level or a character's costume to turning the volume up or down.

How Do You Become a Programmer?

Education

No matter what their specialty, an ideal field of study for would-be programmers is computer science. As the Game Career Guide website notes in the article "Game Programming: An Introduction," "Programmers are math and science people, and more specifically, algebra, calculus, and computer science people. Typically, programmers hold a degree in (or have advanced knowledge of) computer science." Most colleges and universities offer computer science degree programs. The top four schools for computer science, according to the *U.S. News & World Report*, are Carnegie Mellon University, the Massachusetts Institute of Technology, Stanford University, and the University of California, Berkeley, although there are many other similar programs in universities throughout the United States. These four-year programs introduce students to the core concepts of game design, including classes in programming, story and character development, visual and sound design, and game engine development. Earning a degree in computer science exposes would-be programmers to information about various operating systems, programming concepts, input/output methods, and algorithms.

According to O*NET, about 78 percent of general computer programmers have a bachelor's degree, 11 percent have a postsecondary certificate, and 6 percent have only a high school diploma or equivalent. AI specialists typically have a master's degree or a doctorate in computer science or cognitive science.

Certification

Certification in a variety of programming languages is a must; and programmers today are typically expected to have fluency in C++, STL, OpenGL, PhysX, Perl, Perforce, Python, and XML. As the Game Career Guide notes in "Game Programming: An Introduction," "Before programmers find work in the game industry, they need to have a firm and working grasp of a programming language, usually C++, though many also need to know Assembly, C, or Java. C++ is the most common language used in the game industry today."

Getting Experience

Even for people just starting out as game programmers, experience matters. Fortunately, there are many ways to get experience, although most of them require individual initiative. As Aleissia Laidacker, lead game play and AI programmer at Ubisoft Montreal, noted during an April 2016 interview with the We Are Game Devs website, one of the best ways to get noticed by video game developers and companies looking to hire is to code your own game and take part in game developer gatherings:

> Make your own game. With Unity3D [a game development program] it's so accessible to anybody, and Game Jams are a great way to spend 48 hours of your time to come out with a game prototype. I tend to favor applicants with personal projects, game jam experience, hackathons, etc., rather than someone with just good grades. Passion for wanting to get into games and showing that you've spent some time working on your own projects is what I look for most.

Skills and Personality

One of the most important personality traits for programmers is flexibility. Since they will be required to write code or script in a variety of different programming languages, as well as work with a team of fellow programmers, artists, and designers, adaptability is key. Strong written and verbal communication skills are also necessary, along with critical thinking skills. The Game Career Guide suggests that

> programmers must be able to seek out the answers to questions they have and the solutions to problems they face. In this sense, programmers must be strong independent learners. However, it's crucial that game programmers also know how to communicate effectively with others, as their jobs require that they share their knowledge on an everyday basis.

Programming is one of the most technical jobs in any video game company, but it is also a highly creative endeavor. Many programmers regard their ability to write in multiple computer languages to be a kind of art form. As Gil Fewster, a self-described "tinkerer" and freelance programmer, explains in an article on the website freeCodeCamp,

> People who don't code rarely believe this but, for all of its technical rules and structural discipline, programming is a richly creative activity. . . . No two programmers will ever produce identical code, not even if the

final software appears from the outside to be the same. . . . Give ten programmers a functional specification and each one will produce something unique, an expression of their own voice as a programmer.

On the Job

Employers

Most video game programmers are full-time, salaried workers employed by video game companies, which can be large organizations that are easily recognized by avid gamers or smaller ones that release games made for specific mobile platforms. Many programmers work for leading gaming companies like Ubisoft, Nintendo, EA Games, and Blizzard Entertainment. According to a Game Career Guide interview with Gamelab founder Peter Lee, employers are most interested in hiring applicants who are able to see things through to completion, whether it is a computer science degree or a game on which they have begun working. "I see too many recent graduates lacking the capability to create a complete application no matter how small it is," says Lee.

Working Conditions

The workday for programmers can be long, especially when they are designing a new game. Sometimes they spend an entire day just working on bug fixes with other team members. Even after the game is done, the team often moves on quickly to the next project. In a 2016 interview with We Are Game Devs, Laidacker described her typical workday:

> My day for one, starts with coffee . . . lots of it. And then our team usually gets together in the morning to discuss the goals for the day. . . . My role is to see if any [things] need to be fixed, and to work with the team to come up with priorities, roadmaps and next steps. But it really depends at what point I'm at in my project. Some days I'll be in a room with Post-Its everywhere, working with the team to come up with ideas for our

next system we are working on. Sometimes I'm working on design docs. Sometimes I have my headphones on coding all day.

Earnings

The salary of video game programmers depends on the type of company they work for and on their skills and experience. At one end of the spectrum are beginning programmers, who earn about $77,550 a year. At the other end are more advanced programmers, who can earn up to $92,000 per year. O*NET and the Bureau of Labor Statistics (BLS) group video game programmers in with general computer programmers and software engineers, who earned a median salary of $79,530 in 2015. According to information obtained by the job search website Indeed in July 2016, typical video game programmers make an average of $102,000 per year.

Opportunities for Advancement

Different types of programmers will have different experiences within the video game industry, depending on their specialty. AI programmers, for instance, can advance in the field by obtaining a master's degree or a doctorate as well as by working their way up from C++ programmer or junior software engineer. They may also be interested in making the jump from the video game industry into research groups focused on AI, or they may start their own companies to focus on a pet project. AI programmers can also find work in the robotics, voice-recognition, machine vision systems, and natural language industries. No matter what their specialization, programmers must continue to advance their skills and knowledge of the tools and programming languages used in the video game industry. The more they hone their skills, and add years of experience to their résumés, the more in demand they will become, with an accompanying bump in pay to match.

What Is the Future Outlook for Programmers?

Video game programmers face some difficult realities. The BLS predicts that the number of computer programmer jobs will decline by

8 percent through 2024, due to the outsourcing of jobs to countries where the average programmer can be paid much less than a programmer in the United States. As a result there are 26,500 projected jobs that will be lost during this time period. However, the BLS does not collect data specifically on the video game industry—which is one of the fastest-growing segments of the tech world.

Likewise, as consumers continue to seek out newer, more complicated games—including those in the emerging realm of virtual reality (VR)—the skills of competent, experienced programmers will be required. As author Caroline Zaayer Kaufman notes in an October 2015 article on the job search website Monster, "Demand for job candidates with VR knowledge is up 37% over last year . . . and because the technology is new, companies are having difficulty meeting that demand." So although lower-level programming jobs may continue to be outsourced, experienced lead programmers, AI programmers, and others who can create these more complicated games will be in a better position to find jobs.

Find Out More

Association for the Advancement of Artificial Intelligence
www.aaai.org

The AAAI is a nonprofit scientific society devoted to advancing the scientific understanding of the mechanisms of underlying thought and intelligent behavior and their embodiment in machines. This group hosts a yearly conference for those interested in learning more about AI as well as a variety of symposiums throughout the year.

Entertainment Software Association
www.theesa.com

This American association is dedicated exclusively to serving the business and public affairs needs of companies that publish computer and video games for video game consoles, handheld devices, personal computers, and the Internet. The group also hosts an annual trade show for those interested in learning more about new video games and products.

Road to VR
www.roadtovr.com

This is the world's largest independent news publication dedicated to the consumer virtual reality industry. Students can learn much more about virtual reality games and how to create them on this site.

Silicon Valley Virtual Reality (SVVR)
www.svvr.com

SVVR is a fast-growing community of developers, entrepreneurs, hackers, and artists dedicated to advancing affordable and accessible virtual reality and promoting a healthy, diverse VR ecosystem. Students can find local maker spaces and hackathons where they can get involved with virtual reality in their own backyards.

Sound Designer

Sound designers create the audio world of a video game. They build a library of noises and auditory cues that occur during game play—much like the Foley artists of film and television. Working in concert with creative directors, game designers, producers, and other members of the game development team, the sound designer learns more about the setting, characters, and story to create an immersive aural environment for the game. According to an article on the Designing Sound website by sound designer Aaron Marks,

What a lot of people don't know outside of the games industry is that sound designers are still expected to not only be able to craft appropriate sound effects but to also be a field recordist to capture specific sounds to use as elements or as realistic sound effects, be a Foley artist to create specific movement and object handling sounds to follow gameplay or for a game's cinematics [movie-like scenes used to introduce new characters or otherwise break up play], be an audio editor to edit

At a Glance:
Sound Designer

Minimum Educational Requirements
High school diploma or associate's degree

Personal Qualities
Creative problem solver; musically inclined; self-directed; calm under pressure

Working Conditions
Indoors

Salary Range
About $41,780 to $68,000

Number of Jobs
As of 2014 about 117,200

Future Job Outlook
Growth rate of 7 percent through 2024

and manipulate audio elements as needed . . . and perform post-production duties such as synchronizing sounds to their corresponding actions in the game or cinematic.

Although most players probably do not realize it, video games contain a surprising array of sounds. These include noises made by vehicles, imaginary creatures, and weapons. Sound designers may also produce short musical patterns to guide players through different scenes or supply other sounds to indicate whether a puzzle is being solved correctly or steps are being done out of order. There are several different types of sound designs used in most video games; they include ambient sound, effects, music, and voices. It is the sound designer's responsibility to come up with these sounds and also to smoothly integrate them into the game.

Designers may choose to use existing audio files from their own libraries or various open sources, or they may work to create sounds through a combination of real-life recordings, audio mixing, and digital manipulation. As the website Get In Media describes a sound designer's duties,

> The sound designer first must identify the key qualities of the game that will influence his or her design: These include story, location, characters, environment, creatures, vehicles, weapons, and the overall style of the game. Game writers will supply whatever written material has been produced to guide the story's progression, as well as the script for cinematics. With a rough idea in mind of what the game should sound like, the designer returns to his or her own studio to begin breaking down the game into detailed categories of sound effects, voices, ambient sound, and music. Every game will have a different set of requirements, but generally, the designer is concerned with creating or supervising the creation of all audio assets. He or she sifts through catalogs of existing audio files that may suit the game, and engineers supplemental sounds as needed. Games that include a heavy inventory of

weapons or vehicles often necessitate going into the field to record real-life audio that is later manipulated to produce a unique effect for the game.

How Do You Become a Sound Designer?

Education

Sound designers do not typically require any specific degrees in order to get their foot in the door. For those who do choose to study sound, high school courses in math, physics, and electronics will help pave the way; and a degree or certificate in audio engineering or recording arts will also build skills. According to O*NET, about 31 percent of sound engineering technicians have a high school diploma or equivalent, 25 percent have a postsecondary certificate, and 22 percent have an associate's degree. More important than college coursework, sound designers should have a strong command of audio editing software like Logic or Pro Tools as well as familiarity with recording and mixing hardware, which can be learned through free online classes or during internships. The Get In Media website also recommends that a "sound designer should understand the constraints of current-generation game platforms, as well as the capabilities of multiple game engines. Knowledge of audio editing software like Pro Tools is required, as is proficiency with recording and mixing consoles."

Volunteer Work and Internships

Volunteer work or internships at a recording studio would be an ideal fit for anyone considering sound design as a career. Learning how to record, mix, and manipulate sounds in the booth will give aspiring sound designers all of the educational training they need. Access to expensive equipment is also a huge plus since it can be hard to obtain familiarity with the devices professionals are using outside of a studio setting.

Any experience in the field is good experience—even if it is unpaid. Would-be sound designers should be able to demonstrate their abilities with a show reel or portfolio of sounds they have designed. In an article on the Gamasutra website, sound designer Mark Kilborn advises aspiring sound designers to keep videos or sound clips short:

"90-180 seconds. Put your best stuff first. . . . Assume you have about 10 seconds to hook them." Kilborn also suggests including "a cue sheet of some sort, explaining what you did. . . . If for a video, it should have times. If it's for something interactive, then just an explanation that makes sense."

Skills and Personality

The most successful sound designers blend creativity and technical know-how. Inventing entire audio worlds requires a special kind of ability to listen to real-life sounds and manipulate them in order to represent fictional characters and interactions. This means that sound designers must be both musically inclined and able to think outside the box when it comes to blending and distorting sounds for clever solutions to audio problems. "Not only must the designer have the ability to create balanced, quality sound, he or she should also have the creative talent to imagine an entirely new aural world, like the unique sound of a light saber or a dinosaur wail," says Get In Media.

At some stages in the game development process, sound designers work on their own in a studio setting; at other stages, they interact with team members. So they must be both self-directed and able to work well with other people. For instance, a sound designer will work with other team members to make sure all sounds match the game's visual elements.

On the Job

Employers

Hiring managers and producers for leading game companies like Ubisoft, Nintendo, EA Games, and Blizzard Entertainment are in charge of hiring sound designers. In a Gamasutra article aimed at applicants for sound design jobs, Kilborn notes that aspiring designers should always be working on something they can put in their portfolios—particularly something interactive. His advice to designers is, simply, "Always be making noise." Sound designer and blogger Kris Giampa also recommends working on as many indie games as possible in an effort to break into the big game companies.

Working Conditions

Sound designers in the video game industry typically work in a sound studio rather than at the company's headquarters. This may be a production company studio. Or, for freelancers, it might be a home studio. Long workdays, especially as deadlines near for completing a new game, are not uncommon. Raison Varner, an in-house senior sound designer at Gearbox Software, describes his workdays in an interview with the website Careers in Music: "In a low cycle I'll have fairly normal eight-hour days at a relaxed pace. In a peak cycle, I'll have eight-hour high intensity days for a while and then nine to 12-hour high intensity days for a week or two preceding a major milestone. Depending on the milestone, I'll sometimes work a couple of Saturdays or a weekend or two in a row."

A typical day for a sound designer in the game industry can have a lot of variety. Varner continues:

> In the mornings I go through emails, bug tracking notifications, attend lead meetings if I'm a lead on the project or sometimes I need to just immediately jump into content development. Issues will come and go during the day; we may get news that makes us reorient the entire department's priorities. Other times I'm just head down working on a creature, maybe [creating] a voice processing chain [a series of hardware or software effects to create a desired outcome] or implementing a number of sounds into a boss fight. Occasionally I'll spend entire days in meetings, speaking with composers, developing outsourcing plans and schedules. Some of my favorite days are when I'm head down, working on music and everything is just coming together nicely and no fires popped into existence!

Earnings

The salary of video game sound designers depends on the amount of experience and technical proficiency they have obtained in the field. According to the Bureau of Labor Statistics, at one end of the spectrum are entry-level junior sound designers, who earn about $41,780 a year. At the other end are more experienced sound designers who earn about $63,340 per year (although the job search website Indeed showed the average annual salary for a sound designer in July 2016 was $68,000 per year).

Opportunities for Advancement

As sound designers begin to work in the field, they will often apprentice as interns or junior sound designers, working their way up the career ladder to becoming full-fledged sound designers as they progress. After several years in the industry, they can move on to become senior sound designers or audio directors. Additionally, freelance sound designers may be able to join a company as an in-house designer. Other opportunities for sound designers include lateral moves toward becoming composers, recording engineers, or producers.

What Is the Future Outlook for Sound Designers?

Sound designer jobs in the video game industry can be difficult to get. It is a very competitive area of the industry. As sound designer Will Morton warns in a 2015 interview on the Game Career Guide website,

> Before applying for a job in game audio, make sure you REALLY REALLY REALLY want to do it. There are far more people trying to get these jobs than there are jobs available, so you're in a flooded market. Be sure this is what really motivates you to get out of bed in the morning. If you just think it "might be cool" or that it's "better than a normal job," then go do something else.

With a projected 7 percent growth rate through 2024, however, the number of jobs is still increasing, and quality sound designers with a wide range of skills and experience will always be in demand.

Sound designers who maintain and expand their technical proficiency will become more in demand as digital music creation continues to evolve and the accompanying technology also changes. Staying up-to-date with both formal and informal methods of continuing education, including online courses and self-directed study, will help sound designers maintain that cutting edge.

Find Out More

AudioNewsRoom
www.audionewsroom.net

AudioNewsRoom is an online music technology magazine featuring news, software reviews, hardware reviews, and exclusive interviews with makers, developers, and artists. Students can learn a lot about the industry by studying the articles on this site.

Game Sound Design
www.gamesounddesign.com

This informative site offers accurate information on designing sound for video games. There are plenty of how-to articles here as well as inspirational pieces to help aspiring sound designers improve their craft.

Music Radar
www.musicradar.com

This is a popular website for musicians, featuring instrument reviews, how-to articles, advice, and opinion pieces for aspiring digital musicians and sound designers.

Recording
www.recordingmag.com

Recording is a magazine that features reviews, interviews, how-to articles, and much more information for aspiring musicians and sound designers.

Technical Support Specialist

Technical support specialists, also known as customer service technicians or help-desk support, are the people who receive and respond to phone calls from players who are experiencing technical difficulties. In other words, these are the kind souls that help talk angry gamers down from the ledge when a game experiences glitches, freezes up, or otherwise malfunctions during play. These gaming first responders are there to talk gamers through emergencies and crises with their games and to prevent them from leaving negative reviews on various websites. Technical support specialists may also answer questions via live chat and respond to e-mails from consumers seeking assistance.

Usually, technical support specialists will be assigned to a team that covers one or two games at a larger game company

At a Glance:
Technical Support Specialist

Minimum Educational Requirements
Bachelor's or associate's degree

Personal Qualities
Customer service skills; problem-solving skills; strong written and oral communication skills; calm under pressure

Certification and Licensing
Suggested

Working Conditions
Indoors

Salary Range
About $39,000 to $106,310

Number of Jobs
As of 2015 about 766,900

Future Job Outlook
Growth rate of 12 percent through 2024

to ensure that all specialists can properly answer questions about their titles. Although some problems may be relatively easy to resolve—with scripted instructions for walking the caller through each step—other glitches must be resolved by writing special code to move beyond the error. All information provided by the caller must be inputted into a database that records errors in the game, which is then passed along to the quality assurance (testing) department for further resolution. In essence, technical support specialists are customer support troubleshooters. The website Get In Media describes the duties of a technical support specialist:

> Many times, the tech can simply talk the player through a series of simple steps to correct the glitch. In other cases, as with online games, the technician will have network access to enter the customer's profile and make the hard patches necessary to alleviate the trouble. Under all circumstances, the CS [customer service] technician is given a written operating procedure that details the established process for addressing every type of glitch.

If and when a glitch arises that is not covered by standard procedures, the tech support specialist may have to come up with his or her own fix—or report the problem to other departments.

Additionally, as video games continue to expand to the mobile market, new opportunities—and challenges—arise for technical support specialists. As Gartner research director Brian Blau notes in an article on the website Parature, "As mobile devices (smartphones and tablets) continue to grow, the mobile game category will show the biggest growth due to the entertainment value provided by games compared with other app categories." Unfortunately, this may present difficulties for tech support representatives, who may not yet be receiving proper training for mobile-specific issues and glitches. Indeed, additional complications are sure to arise as technical support specialists must now ask players even more screening questions to determine whether they are playing the game on a mobile device, computer, or dedicated console and then study the specific problems that appear for each individual platform. Issues may even appear on

A tech support specialist assists a player who is experiencing technical difficulties during game play. These specialists often deal with people who are frustrated and angry, so they have to be patient and good listeners in addition to possessing technical knowledge of the game.

one gaming platform, but not another, due to the way that the game is formatted, leading to more customer service headaches for technical support specialists.

How Do You Become a Technical Support Specialist?

Education

Technical support specialists do not necessarily require a degree in computer science, game design, or information science in order to be successful, but these types of degrees certainly help with a general understanding of video games and computer systems. They also look good to potential employers. According to O*NET, which classifies technical support specialists as either computer network specialists or computer user support specialists, about 47 percent of computer network support specialists have a bachelor's degree, 22 percent have an associate's degree, and 14 percent have had some college courses but hold no degree. Comparatively, about 29 percent of computer user support specialists hold a bachelor's degree, 22 percent have had some college but hold no degree, and 18 percent hold an associate's degree.

Certification and Licensing

Certification may be required, depending on the company. An A+ certification from the Computer Technology Industry Association is often requested, which certifies grounding in both technology and customer service skills. Other types of certification that may be required include programs offered by Apple, Microsoft, Cisco, and Linux that are specific to these computer operating systems.

Skills and Personality

Technical support specialists rely on their customer service skills to interact with angry, frustrated gamers. Therefore, two of their most important traits are patience and understanding. Paired with excellent active listening skills, they need to be able to quickly understand the problems users describe over the phone or via instant messaging. Likewise, they must ask good follow-up questions in order to help clear up any confusion. A calm demeanor is essential, particularly during heated interactions.

Problem-solving skills are another key trait for tech support. Both simple and more difficult problems arise on a daily basis. For routine questions, the tech support specialist can usually rely on scripted responses. For less common and more difficult issues, specialists need to have an open mind to come up with possible solutions.

Communication skills are also important. Technical support specialists must be able to verbally communicate their solutions to consumers in a clear, concise manner. Strong written communication skills are essential for writing up reports on individual issues to pass along to the quality assurance team and when writing e-mails or live chat messages in response to gamers. As the website Get In Media notes,

As a problem solver that is tasked with troubleshooting technical glitches and with appeasing the customer, the individual in this role should have a solid understanding of game systems, as well as excellent interpersonal skills. A college degree in computer science or game design is beneficial. The customer service technician must be familiar with the systems of the game engine and console platform, as well as multiple computer browsers and network configurations for PC and Mac gaming. Additionally, this position demands a person who can demonstrate strong conflict resolution skills, organization, and focus.

On the Job

Employers

Most technical support specialists are shift workers, who work on-site at large video game companies, such as Blizzard, EA Games, Nintendo, and Ubisoft. They may also be contracted out by staffing companies or hired as temporary or seasonal employees to help out during busier times of year. An August 2016 ad for a virtual gaming support representative on the job search website Indeed suggests that many tech support jobs are actually work-from-home opportunities for applicants with the right skills and technical setups. The job description suggests the following requirements for applicants:

> Excellent Internet connectivity: access speeds of 5 Mbps upload and 7 Mbps download—the faster the better (wireless and/or satellite Internet Service Providers are not compatible with our systems). Productive work environment with one 20-inch monitor, headset, in-house network, and a hard wired Internet connection capable of continuously supporting outstanding call quality and high speed response rate. Headset requirements: USB, dual ear, noise cancelling microphone.

Working Conditions

Technical support technicians are often scheduled twenty-four hours a day, seven days a week, in order to quickly respond to players' questions. Therefore, aspiring tech support workers should have flexibility when it comes to scheduling since they may be asked to work early mornings, late nights, or weekends to help cover all the shifts. As an article on customer service in the gaming industry from the 5CA website notes, "The need for technical support & customer care in the game industry is evolving exponentially and gamers are known to be some of the most demanding customers." Technical support specialists who work for large companies usually work in a call center. The typical call center consists of a large room or rooms filled with cubicles in which workers answer calls from customers. Working in a call center can be stressful, given the lack of privacy and personal space typical in most cubicle setups. Tech support is often seen as the lowest rung on the ladder for most video game companies, and therefore workers may be crammed into what is often referred to as the boiler room, with no assigned seating or particular order to the chaos. Desks may be randomly assigned or given based on seniority.

Additionally, technical support workers are traditionally heavily monitored by supervisors, with calls being recorded for quality assurance purposes. These calls are occasionally monitored by the head of the department, to ensure that all technicians are performing their jobs properly. That being said, working in a call center can also have its perks, such as snacks and meals while on duty and occasional freebies from the company to boost morale.

Earnings

Depending on experience, technical proficiency, and customer service skills, the earnings of technical support specialists may vary widely. According to O*NET, the average computer user support specialist's median income for 2015 was $48,620, and median income for computer network support specialists was $62,250. The highest 10 percent in both categories earned anywhere from $81,260 to $106,310. According to information obtained by Indeed in July 2016, typical technical support specialists make an average of $39,000 per year.

Opportunities for Advancement

Although technical support specialist is an entry-level position with little room for moving up the corporate ladder, the experience gained in this position can lead to other jobs in the gaming industry. Two areas of the industry where tech support experience can come in handy are quality assurance (which involves game testing) and online community management (which involves interaction with players to gather feedback and reward loyal players). As the Get In Media web-site notes, tech support specialist is "typically an entry-level position with a low starting salary, but the job does come with the benefit of getting your foot in the door with a game company.... There is a great deal that you can learn while acting as a CS tech, and the knowledge about the systems and titles the company produces can prove invaluable during an interview for a better gig."

What Is the Future Outlook for Technical Support Specialist?

Technical support specialists will always be in demand as they are frequently the only interaction many players will ever have with a video game company. Some companies have outsourced these jobs to other countries, where the pay scale is much lower than in the United States. On the other hand, a recent *USA Today* article notes that many companies have started to bring these jobs back into the country after receiving customer complaints about the service they received from overseas call centers. Additionally, since part of the job requires a familiarity with the company's games, there is an advantage to keeping this job in-house. The Bureau of Labor Statistics, which considers technical support specialists to be computer support specialists, predicts that this field will grow 12 percent through 2024—which is faster than average for all occupations—and employment of support specialists in computer systems design is expected to grow by 31 percent.

Find Out More

Tech Republic
www.techrepublic.com

This site offers blogs, community forums, vendor reports, software downloads, webcasts, and research for information technology professionals. This site is full of technical information that will appeal to anyone interested in cybersecurity, computer networks, and the ever-expanding world of high-tech gizmos and gadgets.

Tech Support Guy
www.techguy.org

Tech Support Guy hosts free forums for online computer help. This is a perfect place to start for anyone interested in finding—or solving—computer problems.

Tom's Hardware
www.tomshardware.com

This site is a good place to find out more about the computer hardware and peripherals most people use every day. It features how-to articles, reviews of assorted computer hardware, and opinion pieces on technology.

Tom's IT Pro
www.tomsitpro.com

This site includes buying guides, product reviews, news analysis, how-to articles, and case studies around vital technology in business. It is a great source for information about information technology businesses and services.

Animator

Video game animators help bring games to life by portraying on-screen movement and behaviors in a fictional world. Their job is to make sure characters, objects, and scenery—essentially anything that appears on-screen—move appropriately within the context of the game and the platforms on which it is played. As the website Creative Skillset notes, animators must find the best ways to create both functional and cost-effective animations, with respect to the game's technological and platform limitations. Since many motions will be repeated throughout game play, animators build up libraries of movements for each character, which help to create balance between seamless movement and optimizing the game's performance on different platforms. Some of these will have to be coded or keyed by hand, whereas others may be more quickly produced and reproduced with the help of animation software.

Animators frequently work with programmers and artists to make sure their work is presented smoothly, depending on the platform on which the game

At a Glance:
Animator

Minimum Educational Requirements
Bachelor's or associate's degree

Personal Qualities
Critical thinking; active listening; strong written and oral communication skills; complex problem solving; team player

Certification and Licensing
Suggested

Working Conditions
Indoors

Salary Range
About $63,970 to $215,000

Number of Jobs
As of 2014 about 64,000

Future Job Outlook
Growth rate of 5 to 8 percent through 2024

A video game animator helps bring an on-screen fictional world to life. The animator's job is to make sure that characters, objects, scenery, and all action move appropriately within the context of the game and the platforms on which it is played.

appears (mobile, computer, console, etc.). Creative Skillset describes a video game animator's job: "Game production is collaborative and Animators work as part of the art department team. Using the objects, models, and most importantly, characters created by 3D Artists, Animators define their movements and behaviors and apply them using the animation tools and techniques provided by the selected 3D animation software package."

Rigging and skinning individual characters, a process similar to building a skeleton, is one of the animator's main tasks and involves the use of computer modeling programs. Depending on the type of game, animators may be working with two- or three-dimensional (2-D or 3-D) images, each of which requires different types of computer manipulations to give the desired effects. Lifelike effects are achieved by tinkering with colors, textures, light and shadow, and even transparency within the game's world. Hilda Karugabira, a principal animator at Zynga, described her work in a July 2016 interview on the We Are Game Devs website: "Most of my day is spent on animating characters in Maya and integrating them into our game using Unity, working out any bugs. Once in awhile I have to do JSON [JavaScript Object Notation] data stuff in Sublime, and sometimes rigging."

How Do You Become an Animator?

Education

Video game animators typically study computer animation in order to obtain a bachelor's or associate's degree. According to Game Designing.org, the top five schools for game design are the University of Southern California, Carnegie Mellon University, the University of Utah, the DigiPen Institute of Technology, and the Rochester Institute of Technology. It is important to note, however, that the animation of video games requires a different skill set than animation for film or television, and therefore students ought to consider a program with industry-specific training. According to O*NET, 62 percent of video game animators have a bachelor's degree, 19 percent have an associate's degree, and 17 percent have had some college courses but no degree.

Certification and Licensing

Animators may require game programming certification, which typically involves taking four or five classes in game mathematics, 3-D graphics programming, game engine architecture, C++ programming, basic physics, game development, and computer animation. There are online courses that offer these certificates, so students can study at their own pace, although a high-speed Internet connection is required.

Volunteer Work and Internships

Internships are often a requirement for students majoring in animation programs. These offer a great opportunity to learn on-the-job skills as well as network with potential employers. EA Games offers an annual art and animation internship/co-op program for students currently enrolled in bachelor's or master's programs for fine art, visual art, studio art, computer animation, interactive entertainment, illustration, or related fields. Blizzard Entertainment also offers summer internships in animation for juniors in college as well as talented freshmen and sophomores.

In addition, new animators may want to take on volunteer work in order to help build experience. Although some animators may balk at the idea of giving their work away for free, the catch-22 is that companies do not want to take a chance on an untrained animator and yet many of the skills required for becoming proficient are obtained on the job. Therefore, volunteer work provides a straightforward way to obtain experience in the field while simultaneously building a portfolio that can become a bridge to paid work.

An online portfolio, or show reel, is a sampling of one's work—and it is something that prospective employers will want to see. Reels are samples from an animator's creative work, detailing their specific contributions, and typically run two to three minutes long. Potential employers watch reels to see how well animators can portray their characters' personalities through both simple and complex movements, and also look for different genres and styles illustrated. As Ubisoft's lead animator, Patrick Beaulieu, explains in an interview with Animation Arena,

> Concerning a portfolio, they like to see original animations [that] avoid all clichés or movement[s] that are often used or seen everywhere. Only put your best stuff in a demo. It's better to have three good animations than fifteen bad ones. Make a good selection of clips[.] A bit of variety is always interesting[.] For example[:] cartoon, realistic, acting lip sync. . . . When I interview potential candidates, these are some of the things I look for and I'm always surprised.

Skills and Personality

Some of the most important personality traits for video game animators actually revolve around soft skills rather than technical expertise. The ability to coordinate with a group of designers, programmers, and artists who are all working on the same project is important, as are skills like active listening, critical thinking, and communication. Beaulieu explains that "the duties of a Lead Animator are diversified." He notes that not only are lead animators expected to do their own animation work, but they are also required to advise and support other members of the team. Mentoring team members as artists is as important to Beaulieu as making sure the animation is being done in a consistent style across the team. Being patient, understanding, and helpful is just part of the job.

In addition to being patient and understanding, animators must also have effective time-management skills, which are critical when working on a deadline. Whether working with others in a group or working solo, animators must budget their time accordingly in order to meet multiple deadlines and keep projects moving forward. Those who can stay on top of these deadlines will ultimately be considered more valuable team members and will advance more quickly in their careers.

Animators must also constantly deal with complex problems in their own work. Being able to take responsibility for these errors, as well as solve technical and design problems, will help move the project forward. Problem solving is a key trait that most jobs in the video game industry share, as each game is made up of a huge number of complex bits and pieces and many different contributions made by various team members.

On the Job

Employers

Most video game animators are full-time, salaried workers employed by video game companies, which can be large organizations that are easily recognized by avid gamers or smaller companies that release games made for specific mobile platforms. Many work for leading gaming companies like Ubisoft, Nintendo, EA Games, and Blizzard.

Working Conditions

Video game animators typically work with many different types of computer programs, ranging from computer-aided design software, video and graphics programs, to web development programs like Drupal, DHTML, JavaScript, and PHP. Animators also frequently use specific types of computer animation programs like 3D Studio Max and Maya to render their creations. Part of the job also requires keeping up with industry trends and participation in ongoing continuing education (both on and off the job) as new technology is introduced and developed.

In addition to keeping up with industry standards, animators must keep up with their fellow coworkers in order to continue working together harmoniously. Coworkers end up spending a lot of time together on the job and sometimes even hang out with each other after work, whether formally or informally, as part of the corporate culture. Beaulieu describes his working conditions in an interview with *Animation Arena*:

> Making a video game implies that a lot of people must work together, the game designer, programmers, level designers, 3D artists, etc. Working at Ubisoft is very pleasant and we are well treated even if it's a big company. There are always Happy Hours organized for birthdays, game premiers and other activities. Working on a game is very demanding [and] certain projects require overtime. In general I'm telling you to work hard and come work on a video game; you'll have a ball.

Earnings

The salary of video game animators depends on the amount of experience and technical proficiency they have obtained in the field. According to O*NET, at one end of the spectrum are entry-level multimedia artists and animators, who earn about $63,970 per year and can advance to a higher pay scale with experience. At the other end are more advanced artists who have been in the field longer, who earn about $70,300 per year. According to information obtained by the job search website Indeed in July 2016, typical video game animators make an average of $82,000 per year. Lead animators can earn anywhere from $80,000 to $215,000 a year, depending on seniority.

Opportunities for Advancement

Animators can earn the respect of their peers, acclaim within the industry, and expect a salary raise the longer they work in the field. Typically, animators are considered experienced after working three years in the video gaming industry and may be considered for lead animator positions. There is also some possibility for game animators to make a leap to film and television animation, but the animation processes can differ significantly.

What Is the Future Outlook for Animators?

Although animation jobs can be difficult to obtain due to the significant amount of technical expertise and on-the-job training required, the job outlook for this profession is good. With a growth rate of 5 to 8 percent through 2024, the number of jobs is still increasing, and as pocket gaming on cell phones and portable tablets continues to expand, quality animators will certainly be in demand.

Animators who maintain and expand their technical proficiency will become more in demand as the technology behind video games continues to change. Staying up-to-date with both formal and informal methods of continuing education, including online courses and self-directed study, will help video game animators maintain that cutting edge.

Find Out More

Academy of Interactive Arts and Sciences (AIAS)
www.interactive.org

The AIAS is a nonprofit organization dedicated to the advancement and recognition of the interactive arts with more than twenty thousand members. News and interviews with leaders in the video game industry are sure to inspire.

GamesRadar+
www.gamesradar.com

This global gaming website offers news, reviews, and features on a variety of gaming platforms. Aspiring animators would do well to keep tabs on this site in order to keep up with industry trends and breakout successes.

International Game Developers Association (IGDA)
www.igda.org

An independent, nonprofit organization for game software developers, the IGDA offers news, articles, and forums. This group also touts itself as a great place to network with fellow game developers, which can help aspiring animators break into the business or bring their careers to the next level.

PC Gamer
www.pcgamer.com

The number one computer games authority, PC Gamer offers annual Golden Joystick Awards for consumer favorites. This is a great site for those interested in animating computer games.

3-D Artist

What Does a 3-D Artist Do?

3-D artists, also sometimes known as 3-D modelers, create different types of three-dimensional artwork to bring a game's characters, objects, and environment to life. Although their work is predominantly digital, they may also draw, paint, or sculpt these characters using more traditional media like paper and pencil, watercolors, or clay. 3-D artists may even help produce storyboards—plotting out characters, environments, and story lines—along with the rest of the game's design team. In addition, 3-D artists help model or build 3-D characters based on concept artwork, create environmental surfaces and character skins, and rig character skeletons that animators can map and control. According to Creative Skillset, the job of a 3-D artist is to "build the characters, objects and environments of the game, including life forms, scenery, vegetation, furniture, and vehicles, etc. They need to balance visual richness and detail with the limitations of the game's technology." Similar to the work of animators, 3-D artists must also work to balance

At a Glance:

3-D Artist

Minimum Educational Requirements
Bachelor's or associate's degree

Personal Qualities
Critical thinking; active listening; strong written and oral communication skills; complex problem solving; team player

Certification and Licensing
Suggested

Working Conditions
Indoors

Salary Range
About $63,970 to $70,300

Number of Jobs
As of 2014 about 64,000

Future Job Outlook
Growth rate of 5 to 8 percent through 2024

functionality and cost-effectiveness, blending the two to make sure their work renders correctly on many different gaming platforms.

The work of 3-D artists is never boring because they are always working on something different. With no two days alike, 3-D artist Mark Masters says that he never quite knows what to expect from the job, and that is precisely what he likes about it. In a Digital Tutors article, he says, "As a 3D modeler you will never be able to predict the types of projects thrown your way. There may be times when a studio is recruiting 3D modelers to only model specific items such as characters or sets, but you can never predict when that may be."

How Do You Become a 3-D Artist?

Education

3-D artists typically study fine art, graphic design, or illustration in order to obtain a bachelor's or associate's degree. The top five schools for fine art degrees, according to the *U.S. News & World Report*, are Yale University; Virginia Commonwealth University; the University of California, Los Angeles; the School of the Art Institute of Chicago; and the Rhode Island School of Design. In addition to formal education, it is also important for aspiring 3-D artists to experiment with 3-D modeling software as much as possible. As Jordan Banks, a freelance 3-D artist for the 3-D printing website Shapeways, notes,

> College is a great start because it shows you how to focus your skill. . . . What separated me from my peers was when I got home, I continued to watch tutorial after tutorial to learn the programs more. After no time at all, I started trying things on my own, even changing some things in the book. I thought that watching the tutorials was making me better at modeling and using the software. What I learned was it was not the fact that I was watching tutorials that made me great at modeling, it was the experimenting with the program that made me understand to better manipulate the software.

In addition to software skills, 3-D artists must also have advanced math skills as well as skills particular to the field in which they choose to work. The website Animation Career Review notes that 3-D artists in the video game industry are expected to bring creativity and design skills to the table, but

> other skills may be required depending on where the 3D modeler works. For example . . . 3D modelers in scientific fields may have a strong background in any given area of science. The major and concentration area you choose will depend entirely on the field you wish to enter. For example, if you are interested in becoming a 3D modeler in the game industry, consider majoring in game design.

3-D artists typically work with many different types of computer programs, including 3-D graphics programs such as 3D Studio Max and Maya, sculpting programs like ZBrush and Mudbox, and 2-D programs like Photoshop. Part of the job also requires keeping up with industry trends and participation in ongoing continuing education (both on and off the job) as new technology is introduced and developed.

Certification and Licensing

3-D artists may require game programming certification, which typically involves taking four or five classes in game mathematics, 3-D graphics programming, game engine architecture, C++ programming, basic physics, game development, and computer animation. There are online courses that offer these certificates, so students can study at their own pace, although a high-speed Internet connection is required.

Volunteer Work and Internships

Internships are often a requirement for students majoring in fine art programs, and these offer a great opportunity to learn on-the-job skills as well as network with potential employers. In addition, new 3-D artists will want to take on volunteer work in order to help build up their portfolios. EA Games, for example, offers an art and animation internship/co-op program available to both undergraduate and master's students studying fine art, visual art, studio art, computer animation, interactive entertainment, illustration, or a related field. 3-D artists can certainly learn a great deal from observing and working with fellow 3-D artists during this kind of internship as well as get a feel for the dynamics of group work within the industry.

In addition to pursuing internships, 3-D artists will need to be able to show their work through an online portfolio. (Internships are a great way to get material for a portfolio.) Potential employers want to see the kinds of artwork that an artist has produced as well as the different styles in which the artist is proficient. As 3-D artist Sam R. Kennedy notes in his book *How to Become a Video Game Artist*,

> A portfolio is a selection of examples of your best artwork to show a potential employer your skills, talents, and artistic vision. The artwork can be drawings, digital paintings, 3D models, animation, and/or other graphics. Your portfolio should also be available on the web. The work in your portfolio should visually illustrate the skills needed for the job you're interested in and should also show your proficiency in all software programs required.

Skills and Personality

3-D artists must be both technically proficient and artistically skilled in order to succeed in the video game industry. Aside from artistic skills, some of the most important personality traits for 3-D artists actually revolve around soft skills. The ability to coordinate with a group of designers, programmers, and artists who are all working on the same project is important, as are skills like active listening, critical thinking, and communication. 3-D artists must also be able to monitor themselves and be self-starters to ensure that all deadlines are met. Time-management skills can also be critical when working on studio deadlines.

Aspiring artists need to have realistic expectations. There are a lot of talented people working as 3-D artists in the game industry, and

3-D artists, or modelers, create the three-dimensional artwork that gives life to a game's characters, objects, and environments. Most of their work is digital but they sometimes also draw, paint, or sculpt life-forms, scenery, and other elements of a game.

it is easy for young artists to compare their work to the work of these more experienced artists. Doing that can be overwhelming—and even harmful to a young artist's development. Instead, Jonathan Williamson, a 3-D artist at the 3-D training website CG Cookie, urges young artists to learn all they can from more experienced artists but keep in mind that developing talent and skills takes time. In an article for the i.materialise website, Williamson explains that it is important to

> focus and [avoid] self-judgment. While you're learning 3D modeling . . . there's a lot you need to learn. Take it a step at a time and try not to get overwhelmed or too ahead of yourself. Also, it's very easy to compare yourself negatively to other professionals but you have to keep in mind that most of what you see of other people's work is their successes, whereas you're often judging yourself based on your collective work, including

failures and successes. What you don't see is all the failures that those professionals aren't showing every single day. I forget who first told me that, but it's really stuck with me, particularly while learning new skills.

On the Job

Employers

Most 3-D artists are full-time, salaried workers employed by video game companies, which can be large organizations that are easily recognized by avid gamers or smaller companies that release games made for specific mobile platforms. Many work for leading gaming companies like Ubisoft, Nintendo, EA Games, and Blizzard Entertainment. Some may also be freelancers, who work from home for different companies depending on the projects available.

Working Conditions

A typical workday doesn't exist for most 3-D artists, as they are always working on something different, depending on which stage of the artistic process they're in. In a June 2016 interview with the website We Are Game Devs, Joe Perez described a typical day, saying,

> That's a tough question because it changes all the time. One day I could be working on lighting, another day I'd fix bugs or create new models, or learn something totally new. I love that kind of dynamic; it makes working there way more fun. I typically go in at 9 and finish at 6. We really don't have much crunch, which is maybe a bit weird for the industry, but we have our moments.

Earnings

The salary of 3-D artists depends on the amount of experience and technical proficiency they have obtained in the field. According to O*NET, at one end of the spectrum are entry-level artists, who earn about $63,970 per year and can advance to a higher pay scale with experience. At the other end are more advanced artists who have been in the field longer, who earn about $70,300 per year. According to information obtained by the job search website Indeed in July 2016, typical 3-D artists make an average of $66,000 per year.

Opportunities for Advancement

3-D artists can earn the respect of their peers, acclaim within the industry, and expect a salary raise the longer they work in the field. Typically, artists are considered to be experienced after working three years in the video gaming industry; at that time, they may be considered for senior artist or lead artist positions. There is also some potential for 3-D artists to switch from the video game industry into the film industry, which may bring additional risks and rewards. As the website The Art Career Project points out,

> 3D modeling is a very multi-faceted career that can involve working for a large variety of industries. While many associate 3D with computer animation and filmmaking, this is only one option that a 3D modeler may pursue. In fact, they can work for architecture firms, the health care industry, laboratories, product design, the automotive industry, manufacturing and many others. This is because 3D modeling has become extremely popular in the recent years, since it gives the opportunity to test concept art in a more realistic environment.

What Is the Future Outlook for 3-D Artists?

Although 3-D artist jobs can be difficult to obtain due to the significant amount of technical expertise and on-the-job training required, the profession is projected to grow between 5 and 8 percent through 2024. Those who continually work on updating their skills will maintain their edge within the workforce.

Find Out More

CG Society
www.cgsociety.org

CG Society is a global organization for creative digital artists. Student-animated shorts are featured on the site, along with plenty of 3-D art and workshops.

gamedevmap
www.gamedevmap.com

A living map and catalog of game development organizations, students and aspiring 3-D artists can use the gamedevmap to locate game publishers and studios for potential jobs or internship opportunities.

Pluralsight
www.digitaltutors.com

An online learning center for 3-D animators and artists, this site offers essential tools and online workshops for aspiring 3-D artists.

Polycount
www.polycount.com

This online gallery of 3-D artwork is a great place for aspiring 3-D artists to feature their work and attract potential employers or internship opportunities.

ZBrushCentral
www.zbrushcentral.com

This online forum, classroom, and gallery for 3-D artists should be a daily destination for aspiring 3-D artists in search of information and inspiration.

Quality Assurance Tester

What Does a Quality Assurance Tester Do?

Quality assurance testers (also known as video game testers) locate and report problems with individual video games during the postproduction phase. This is the period after the game is completed but before it is made available to customers. Even the best-designed video games have glitches. The goal of testers is to find all of those glitches—or as many as possible—before the game goes public, but they may also be involved with reproducing player-reported glitches once the game is available to consumers. Testers typically look for bugs in the game's software that take away from the overall user experience. For instance, bugs might cause the game to get stuck at the same point in a certain level, or they may prevent the game from advancing. Testers might also look for art glitches, such as failure to properly render a character or environment. Although quality assurance testers are the

At a Glance:
Quality Assurance Tester

Minimum Educational Requirements
Bachelor's or associate's degree

Personal Qualities
Critical thinking; self-directed; strong written and oral communication skills; calm under pressure

Certification and Licensing
Suggested

Working Conditions
Indoors

Salary Range
About $20,800 to $45,000

Number of Jobs
As of 2015 about 233,000

Future Job Outlook
Growth rate of 2 to 4 percent through 2024

ones who find the glitches, they do not necessarily fix them. When they identify problems in a game, they alert other members of the game development team so that they can fix the problems.

Finding the glitches is not always easy. Often it requires many hours of playing and replaying specific parts of a game in search of problems that a player might encounter. And although part of their work entails playing a game like any gamer, they also use specific testing methods to help root out any problems. For example, they might use matrix testing, which requires playing every character against each of the others in a game at every level. Or they might use functionality testing, which involves testing all of a game's features to make sure they work according to the game's documentation. In addition, once programmers have fixed the reported bugs, quality assurance testers might conduct regression testing, which is the act of retesting levels that have previously been tested.

Sometimes the object of testing is actually to break the game, but other times the goal is simply to play as any ordinary gamer might. When an error, glitch, or potential problem is found, the tester flags the issue, documents it, and alerts the lead tester. Documentation usually involves a written description of the problem, notes about how it can be reproduced, screenshots (particularly for art glitches), and any relationship that the tester may notice between additional errors he or she has already spotted. As Brent Gocke, the senior release manager at Sony Computer Entertainment America, notes in a *Time* magazine interview, "If you enjoy tinkering and trying to break things, video game testing could still be potentially a route for you. It's for someone who is meticulous, someone who enjoys games and is passionate about playing these things and the different possibilities."

How Do You Become a Quality Assurance Tester?

Education

The typical route to becoming a video game tester comes from a love of playing video games, but there are many different skills that ultimately bring people into the world of testing. Although there are no specific educational requirements for game testers, more and more employers do require some formal study, whether in computer programming or a related field. Technical and community colleges offer undergraduate certificates in software quality assurance, which can be completed in as little as six months.

However, those who only hold certificates may find themselves up against tough competition from applicants with bachelor's degrees in more specialized fields, such as computer science, information technology, or software engineering. According to O*NET, about 64 percent of software testers have a bachelor's degree, 14 percent have an associate's degree, and 9 percent have a master's degree. Students who want to advance within the field but do not want to opt for a master's degree can also find graduate certificate programs in software quality assurance, which can be completed in about one year. These programs can also typically be completed while the student works full-time, and course credit can sometimes be transferred toward the pursuit of a master's degree. Master's degree programs are usually in software engineering with a concentration on testing issues.

Additionally, many of the skills required of testers can only be learned on the job. Things like understanding how an application programming interface or a particular gaming company's proprietary software and setups work, for instance, can only be learned with experience.

Certification

Many employers require video game testers to be certified. One of the most common qualifications is the software tester certification offered by the International Software Certification Board. This certification must be renewed every three years, and work experience is required in addition to the written test. Additional certifications that may benefit a quality assurance tester include the certified software quality engineer designation and the certified reliability engineer designation, both offered by the American Society for Quality.

Skills and Personality

Video game testing attracts a specific type of individual. Although most are gaming enthusiasts, the key to being a good tester is enthusiasm for improving the game. But that alone is not enough. Quality assurance testers must also be patient, methodical, and able to work on their own without direct supervision. Testers should be analytical, with the ability to discover problems and offer possible solutions. They also need to have strong written and oral communication skills to describe problems clearly and accurately to other team members. It can also be helpful for testers to analyze problems from a developer's or designer's point of view as well as using a gamer's mind-set. The best testers have a good understanding of how the entire game development process works.

At times, working as a quality assurance tester can be a thankless job. When gamers discover glitches, their reports and complaints usually end up with testers. Sometimes those reports help testers identify missed glitches, but sometimes they are just avid gamers spouting off about features of the game that they do not like. Patience—and the ability to not take criticism personally—are helpful traits in a game tester. On a 2015 "Ask Me Anything" question-and-answer forum on the social media website Reddit, one tester described some of the interaction between gamers and game makers: "Developers get hundreds of suggestions nearly every day from forum posts, Twitter posts, posts on their Facebook pages, sent via in-game support tickets, etc. The *vast* majority of these 'suggestions' are just players complaining without providing any sort of suggestion on how to fix the thing they don't like."

Being able to successfully keep one's cool under pressure is also an important component in video game testing. Testers are required to play through the same portions of a game over and over again, particularly as crunch time (the lead-up to the game's release date) occurs. Testers may also be subjected to up to eighty-hour workweeks during this period in order to make sure the game releases on time. Since the tester's feedback on a game is critical to its success, this pressure can sometimes be overwhelming. The tester's job is an invaluable one, making sure that the consumer's game play experience is the best it can possibly be.

On the Job

Employers

Most quality assurance testers are contract workers who move from project to project. Some are either hired directly or are placed in long-term assignments by information technology recruiting firms. Video game testers work for video game companies, which can be large organizations that are easily recognized by avid gamers or smaller companies that release games made for specific mobile platforms. Many work for leading gaming companies like Ubisoft, Nintendo, EA Games, and Blizzard Entertainment.

Working Conditions

A quality assurance tester usually works independently in an office environment. A lead tester will oversee a quality assurance team, which may range from just a handful of testers in a small company to several hundreds of testers in a large one. Some testers are able to work from home and may telecommute a few days a week. Most testers work full-time. Since game development is often driven by deadlines, it is not uncommon for testers to work long hours. In addition, crunch time may require testers to work overtime and/or night shifts in order to make sure that all bugs at all levels of game play have been located and fixed before the game ships to consumers.

Nonetheless, there are definitely some benefits to working for a company that produces games. As game tester Danny McGee notes in an article on the website Newsvine, working at EA Games included perks like

> free cereal and milk in the break room, in addition to absurdly cheap vending machines (well-stocked with Mountain Dew) and free-to-play arcade games, a company store filled with video games from every EA-owned publisher and developer discounted at more than 50% off, and every once in a while—just for good measure—there are the on-the-clock keg parties complete with free pizza, wings and video game tournaments.

Earnings

Pay for quality assurance testers varies depending on where they live, who they work for, what type of game they are testing, and how much experience they have. According to one source, game testers typically earn about $10 to $18 per hour and are paid hourly rather than being salaried. But another source, the job search website Indeed, states that in June 2016, typical video game testers made an average of $45,000 per year.

Opportunities for Advancement

Even as video game testers gain more experience, there is little opportunity for advancement within the testing realm. Some may be able to attain the more senior-level position of lead tester, but additional opportunities for climbing the corporate ladder are limited. Those who wish to transition to management, design, or programming jobs within the same company will typically need more education in order to break into those roles. Graduate-level management courses would be ideal for those with management-level aspirations, and software design or computer programming degrees would be preferable for those seeking design or programming jobs. Game testers who have advanced testing skills can also become software quality assurance engineers, which are software developers with the ability to write scripts to test complex, specialized software. Whatever angle a tester decides to pursue, the move will be a lateral one rather than a straightforward career progression.

What Is the Future Outlook for Quality Assurance Testers?

Unlike other types of software testing, video game testers will always be required to play through games manually in search of bugs. Since testers must both imitate regular game players and actively seek out ways to break the game in order to improve its performance, there is no real way to automate these positions. Additionally, games must be played with several different goals in mind, something that would be quite taxing for a machine—even one with artificial intelligence. Nonetheless, competition for these jobs is likely to be stiff since there are always plenty of new recruits eager to play video games for a living.

Find Out More

3D World
www.creativebloq.com/3d-world-magazine

3D World is a magazine for game development artists (as well as special effects and television production) featuring interviews with game developers at high-profile companies as well as tips on how to break into the industry.

Gamasutra
www.gamasutra.com

Gamasutra is a website founded in 1997 that is dedicated to "the art and business of making games" and includes articles on all aspects of game development.

Game Career Guide
www.gamecareerguide.com

Game Career Guide is a website affiliated with Gamasutra. It focuses specifically on advice for those seeking careers in gaming.

GameDev.net
www.gamedev.net

This is an online community for game developers of all levels, including professionals, hobbyists, and students.

GamesIndustry.biz
www.gamesindustry.biz

This site covers worldwide breaking news from the game industry. It is part of the Gamer Network.

International Game Developers Association (IGDA)
www.igda.org

The IGDA is a global network of collaborative projects and communities comprising individuals from all fields of game development. Members may be interested in using the site to connect with colleagues in the game industry, and to network to move their careers forward.

Interview with a Game Designer

Sande Chen is currently a freelance writer and game designer. She is also the leader of the Game Design Special Interest Group for the International Game Developers Association and has worked in the video game industry for more than fifteen years. Chen runs the popular game design blog *Game Design Aspect of the Month* and is both a Writers Guild of America- and Grammy-nominated video game designer and writer. She discussed her career with the author via e-mail.

Q: Why did you become a video game designer?

A: Game design was the perfect blend of analytical and creative endeavors for me. It utilized my majors from college, economics, and writing. While a lot of people can see the creative side to design, there is a mathematical part that really appealed to me.

Q: How does math come into play when designing a video game?

A: An understanding of mathematics is needed for game design (and indeed, the whole of game development). Even if we look at a simple game, like a platformer, there is mathematics required for actions like walking or jumping. There is a basis in physics. The mathematics requirement can be very complex, especially for games that require the use of algorithms or AI [artificial intelligence].

Game balance ensures that a game is fun for a player. There needs to be the right level of challenge or the player will find the game too easy and get bored. The player will not be having fun. If the game is too difficult, then the player will get frustrated and may quit the game. Game balance is also about ensuring that there is no golden path to victory. For example, if you have many different kinds of weapons, then the stats of the weapons need to be balanced so that they are all viable choices. If players find that one weapon is overpowered compared to the other weapons, they will only use that weapon. Every aspect of a game needs to have balance, including character stats, combat abilities, reward tables, etc. . . . When it comes to balancing the game, game designers may spend lots of time in front of spreadsheets and manipulating numbers.

Q: Can you describe your typical workday?

A: I work on various projects. Some time is spent on research, which could be viewing YouTube videos, reading reference books, or playing related games. But the bulk of the time is spent on creating documents. Game designers are often the social glue between artists, producers, and programmers. They need to be in good communication with all of these interested parties and get their buy-in to proposed ideas. One important thing about game design documents is getting other people to read them.

Beyond team mechanics, sometimes a game designer is involved in the pitch to publishers or other funders. This kind of game documentation will have to be succinct and understandable to laypeople.

Q: What do you like most and least about your job?

A: What I like most is that because the subject matter from game to game is so varied, I usually end up learning something new about the world. While I may not be faced with a zombie apocalypse any time soon, I can apply the same precautions about sheltering in place to other more plausible situations. What I like least is the public sentiment that I don't have a real job or I must be playing video games all day.

Q: What personal qualities do you find most valuable for this type of work?

A: One should be naturally curious about how systems work, how one thing affects the other, and the interconnectedness of everyday life. Famous [video game] designers like Shigeru Miyamoto take inspiration from daily life.

Q: How do you come up with new game ideas?

A: Game ideas come from anywhere. I mentioned Shigeru Miyamoto previously. *Nintendogs* was inspired when Miyamoto's family got a new puppy. *Pokémon* creator Satoshi Tajiri loved collecting bugs. But all game ideas need to be developed further into a paper prototype or demo so that they can be play tested. Sometimes, the prototype ends up not being fun, so the designer has to try something different with the idea.

Q: What advice do you have for students who might be interested in this career?

A: Play all kinds of games, bad and good. Read books. Know about a lot of things.

Other Jobs in Gaming

Art director
Audio engineer
Audio programmer
Chief executive officer
Cinematic artist
Community manager
Composer
Concept artist
Copywriter
Creative director
Developer
Development and operations
  engineer
Economics designer
Editor
Flash developer
Front-end developer
Kickstarter project organizer/
  leader
Layout artist
Lead artist

Lead programmer
Level designer
Line editor
Motion-capture artist
Musician
Network programmer
Photographer
President
Producer
Professional gamer
Project manager
Proofreader
Publisher
Rotoscope artist
Social media manager
Sound engineer
Studio executive
Technical artist
Tools programmer
Voice-over artist/designer
Writer

Editor's Note: The US Department of Labor's Bureau of Labor Statistics provides information about hundreds of occupations. The agency's *Occupational Outlook Handbook* describes what these jobs entail, the work environment, education and skill requirements, pay, future outlook, and more. The *Occupational Outlook Handbook* may be accessed online at www.bls.gov/ooh.

Index

Picture Credits

About the Author

Laura Roberts writes fiction and nonfiction for young adults and adults. She has worked as a weekly columnist, writing coach, professional book reviewer, and editor; and she has been freelancing since 2007. She lives in San Diego, California, with her husband, Brit.